SEA TURTLES:
FUN FACTS ABOUT TURTLES OF THE WORLD

BABY PROFESSOR

EDUCATION KIDS

Speedy Publishing LLC
40 E. Main St. #1156
Newark, DE 19711
www.speedypublishing.com

Copyright 2018

All Rights reserved. No part of this book may be reproduced or used in any way or form or by any means whether electronic or mechanical, this means that you cannot record or photocopy any material ideas or tips that are provided in this book.

Turtles that live in the
ocean are called sea turtles.

Sea turtles are one of the **Earth's** most ancient creatures. **The** seven species that can be found today have been around for **110** million years.

Turtles have
a hard shell
that protects
them, this upper
shell is called
a 'carapace'.
Turtles also
have a lower
shell called a
'plastron'.

Sea turtles feed
on a wide range
of animals and
plants. They eat
a wide variety
of plant and
animal life,
including insects,
crustaceans,
seagrasses
and worms.

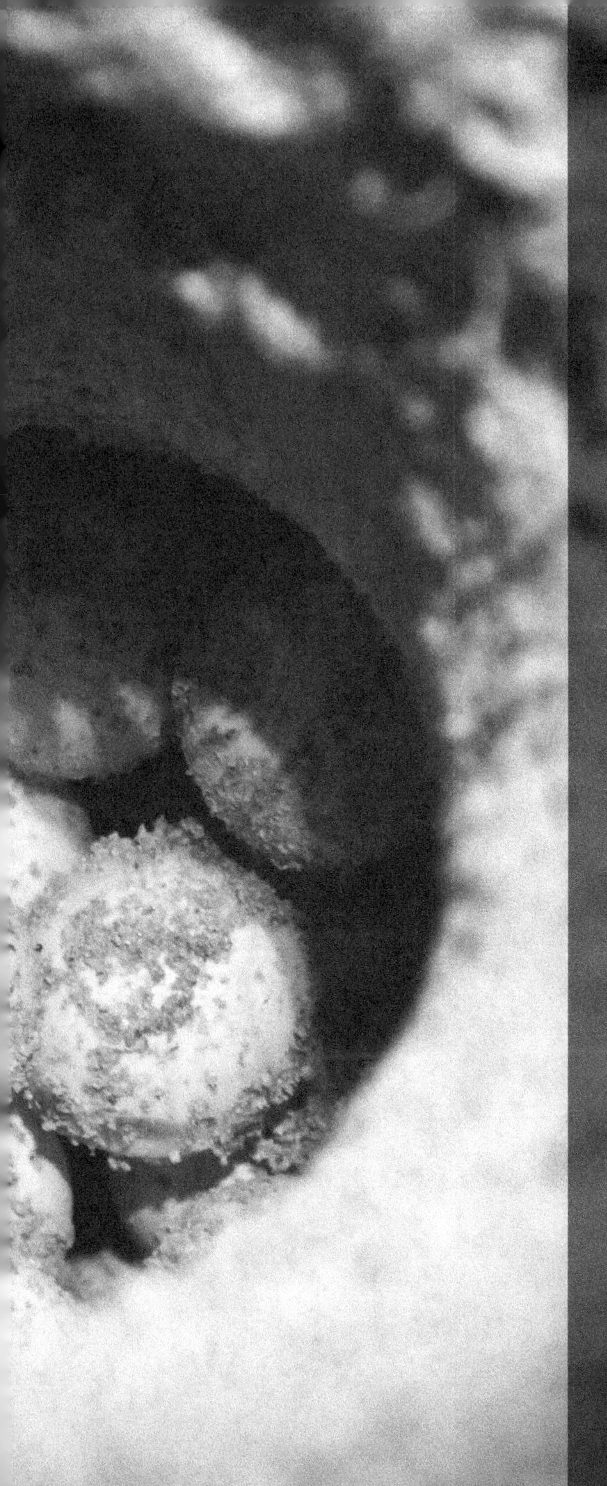

In some species of turtle the temperature determines if the egg will develop into a male or female, lower temperatures lead to a male while higher temperatures lead to a female.

When the young hatch out of their eggs, they make their way to the ocean. They are very vulnerable to predators during this time.

Sea turtles spend most of their lives in the water. Many sea turtles can hold their breath for over 30 minutes.

Sea turtles sometimes look like they are crying. These tears are from special glands which help remove salt from the water they drink.

www.ingramcontent.com/pod-product-compliance
Lightning Source LLC
Chambersburg PA
CBHW080946130726
48003CB00010BA/3116